Foreword

Today is the day I've waited for since my son entered high school. It's the day I have drilled into his head that he *gets* to experience a career and the life he desires. But why does it feel like I'm going home to an empty house with no new possibilities. I mean...I planned my son's life and what it would look like past high school. That was the easy part. But, when I thought about my life and what I would be doing past his graduation, I never envisioned or planned for this time when he left home and started this new chapter. I didn't contemplate what I would do first when I got back home after dropping him off to school.

So now what? What do I do when I get home? Do I cook a three course meal for one? Do I clean the house until it shines? What will I do in the mornings with no one to wake up for school or drop off at the train station? He's not yelling, "Mom come on we're gonna be late!" I sometimes feel like he was the one that kept us on time each day. What do I do when I get off of work? Do I meet friends? Do I *even* have friends that go out during school days? What am I talking about...now that my son is away at college my days are no longer classified as *school* days. My days are now days that I can do anything I want. I can go out to dinner after work come in at 11pm and not worry about any responsibilities at home.

My days can be filled with naps, wine drinking, dates and fun meet-ups after work...that seems like an amazing adult life, right? But why does it feel so foreign and so hard to do? These were the thoughts that ran through my mind as

I drove eight hours back home after leaving my son at his new off campus apartment. I cried mostly for the obvious reasons but as I began to think about going home to an empty house I felt a sense of sadness overwhelm me and fear about what *my life would* look like on a day to day basis now that I have an *Empty Nest.*

Many people experience these feelings after their children have gone off to college or are all grown up, move out and have claimed their independence from us....*AS* they should *but* it hits us like a true loss and we go through many phases of grief before we can get back up and move forward.   If these are your feelings and you have dropped your kids off to college, they have moved out or you may have experienced a divorce, separation and/or you are in a space in your life where you want to re-create you're your sense of self and live a life that is full of fun new experiences and most of all sexiness~ this is the book for you!

This book is designed to help you understand the major life transition you have just gone through and give you as much insight into who you are and as many new ways of experiencing your best

self now as it has given me. It is designed

to help you to understand the sadness

you have just gone through, process these

feelings and look to the new possibilities

life has for you!

Live, love, laugh and be sexy!

~Dina

The house is where we reside?

_____

This book is titled *Empty Nest, Sexy House*
because our house is where we reside. It's
where our inner most desires, passions
and emotions live. We not only reside
within a house but we are the house we
reside in and whatever emotions we have
within our body which houses our spirit
become what we actually experience
within in our life.

Our spirit houses the emotions we have
been imprisoned to due to

disappointment or the grief and despair that we have been at the mercy of *and* have not allowed to heal. Or after healing our spirit we live a full life of excitement, joy and freedom which we have created. We get to choose how we want to live and what feelings we desire to house within our spirit but in this choice we have to work hard to come out of the grief, the despair and the unknown that *life* has offered us.

When I made a choice to heal and go with the uncertainty that was ahead of me; I made a decision to re-create a life for myself after sending my son off to live the life I've prepared for him since he was in grade school. My process started off with many tears and a lack of understanding from those around me because this wasn't something they knew much about. There was an inner feeling that I *should* just be happy and fun would just come my way but this wasn't the case. I had to create this for myself and that was the scary and complex part but, I did it and it was an amazing journey and my desire is that I can support you in your process and journey and prayerfully in a less painful way than mine.

How to use this book?

_____

There are multiple ways in which this book can be experienced. Of course it can be read alone but who wants to do that #nofunatall☹. It would be so much more fun _read_ with a couple of friends whose desire is to be as sexy as YOU'RE going to be within your house; your spiritual house that is. Trust me you are going to be one of the sexiest, socially confident people out here when this is all in the works. It would also help to have accountability partners that can go out

with you, shop with you and cry with you

when it seems like things are not working

out according to plan. Most of all it helps

to have a good support team around you

so even if you read alone find someone

you can share your journey with so with

support they can be your biggest

cheerleader during this new journey

within your life.

Remember to *be kind* to yourself because

as we all know *Rome wasn't built in a day*

and your house (spirit) is your temple

and if your temple is full of judgment you

will become a magnet for it...let's magnify

self-love, patience, excitement and most

of all EMPOWERMENT for our new sexy

house!

Chapter 1

Grief, the normal process
of reacting to a loss...

After my eight hour drive which seemed like the longest drive ever. I arrived at my home and dropped all my bags by the front door. I crawled under the covers and begin my new life as a single woman with an empty nest. A couple of weeks before I left to take my son to college I had two major crises happen, my dog who I've had for eight years died suddenly and my long-term relationship ended which even though I was happy about this relationship ending (juicy story for another book) it was sad to know that I was completely single with no one to comfort me when I returned home from this trip.

and the sadness begins….

I started my new life by laying on my bed, face planted in the pillows and I started to search for a show I'd never seen before on Netflix. I found Grey's Anatomy…jackpot I thought to myself. I can watch this for the day and think about what my next move might be. Well 3 weeks later I was still sitting in the same spot…*literally*. I was eating and sleeping in the same space all while I watch episode after episode of Grey's Anatomy. There were 8 seasons with about 20 episodes in each season and I was on season 6 by the end of week 3. Sad isn't it, I thought the same thing but I was so lost, I was emotional and didn't understand why I was feeling this way instead of feeling alive and free and excited about walking through the house naked (which is what all parents aspire to do when their kids go to college.) Why wasn't I walking around the house in my birthday suit? Not sure of the reason I even wanted to do this, but I wasn't doing any of this.

I wasn't feeling better after 3 weeks so I took off some extra days from work to get myself together. But the longer I stayed in this space, the longer I wanted to hibernate. Crazy thoughts started to run through my mind.   I thought about becoming a foster parent to have someone to come home to...I mean I've always wanted another child so this may be my chance. But I thought to myself "I can't become a parent again because I couldn't wait to be in the space of having zero responsibility before my son went off to college" Girl-bye...I quickly let that idea go.   I thought about getting a roommate and then remembered the time my last roommate stole all of my fitted sheets when she moved out after our huge blow up and again felt like that wouldn't work and wasn't worth the possibility of buying new sheets. I finally decided that I would just take it day by day and see if my friends and coworkers would help me figure it out.

After about 4 weeks, I returned to work and started to talk to my coworkers and friends about what single people do for fun. I mean when I watched TV shows with single people they all look like they are hanging out, having sexy time and drinks with other really cool beautiful single people; but my friends had ideas like "take a pottery class or join a book club" which completely shocked me but made me wonder *more* does this only happen in movies; sexiness and fun times? At the end of my first day back at work I got home and busted into tears the minute I walked into my door. I sobbed for about an hour straight. It was like a wailing cry that happens when you've lost someone you've loved all of your life. Besides this sense of sadness I felt angry confused and frustrated. I decided to give into these feelings and commenced to crying...yeah I actually did because I didn't know what else to do. I knew enough about grief counseling to know that this felt like grief. It sounds weird but it was true I was grieving the loss of my son not being my sole relationship anymore. I was grieving the loss of my old life as a mom who made all decisions for and with my son present. I was a younger mother because I gave birth to my son at the age 18 soon to turn 19 years old and all of my life I made decisions as we all have based on where we would live, what we'll eat daily, morning and night regimens that worked for he and I etc. etc.

I was also grieving the loss of an identity that I got so use to which also at times became the reason why I didn't go out to singles events, go to meet-up groups or travel to exotic countries. I was a single mom and these things didn't fit my life because I had a responsibility which I thought. I took being a mom very seriously, it meant the world to me to raise a responsible and productive young male.

The grievance stage, for most people, is very similar. In grief counseling we go by the acronym DABDA which is experienced as Denial, Anger, Bargaining (gaining understanding,) Depression and Acceptance. I was at the stage of Bargaining which for me during this stage, the best thing to do is to allow yourself to cry, sob and wail most of all allow these feelings to flow through your body so they can't manifest themselves in other ways. Depression, anger or bitterness about life and your new circumstances is a real phase in processing grief and if not allowed can show up in other ways within the body such as sickness, fatigue and digestive problems.

Most people think that grievance happens only when you have lost someone to death but grievance can happen even when you have disconnected from friendships, love relationships and when your children go off to college and start one of the most amazing phases of their lives.

Grief means deep sorrow for a loss, according to Webster's dictionary. Ashley Davis Bush, LCSW wrote an article titled "When your child goes off to College: 4 steps to grieving" and hit the nail on the head when she stated "she held joy and sorrow in her heart simultaneously." This is the exact feelings that you feel; I mean you're of course happy that your child has taken his or her next step in life and they are going to experience the outside world in such a way that it changes their perspective for the better *forever* but you also have sorrow that you must figure out what makes you happy each moment of each day and many of us don't know 5 things off the top of our head that make us happy if asked the question.

As I mentioned earlier depression with sadness is an important stage within the grieving process and if you take the path of least resistance and allow yourself to feel the sadness that comes you will eventually feel better and come out on top. Depression can be scary for many because for some this looks like days full of tears and sorrow. For others it may be scary because you are consumed by feelings that are unexplainable. "What if I can't find my way out of this; what if I fall so deep into depression that I can't come back from it?" This is a question that may lead many people to a place of holding on to their feelings which can be detrimental to your progress and the life that awaits

you as you go through this process.
Finally depression can be scary because
normal crisis management tools don't
seem to be working; like staying busy or
talking to friends because they don't get
it.

It [depression] can also be a
shameful place because people around
you will say "what are you sad about they
just went to school they'll be back."
People rarely understand it unless they
have gone through it themselves, this is
one of those true times that experience
becomes your best teacher.

Grey's Anatomy was a part of my grievance process it gave me solitude when was I sad and something to look forward to when I got home each day. It allowed me to be *with* myself everyday which was important. When I took my time off from work I woke up to what was comfortable to me which was watching this show. I didn't have to be anyone but myself. I didn't have to put on a good face for anyone and I could cry when I needed to without anyone telling me" it'll be ok" or shaming me for feeling what I was feeling at the time.

After about 4 weeks of this sadness I created an understanding in my head about what was happening in my life which was the ending of my Bargaining phase within my grief process when you think about the stages. Acceptance is the step after Bargaining and I was ready for this! I reflected and realized that I have worked really hard to get him into college and he is there *and* this in itself is amazing but now I must figure out what brings me joy, fun, laughter and excitement each day.

So I made a pact with myself that each day I was going to do whatever I decided to do that made me happy. I was going to try new things and I was going to document the things that made me happy by creating a go to list for myself of things that I knew could change my mood anytime and bring me happiness. I started with a celebration dinner with my friends. I invited a few sexy and fun guys and gal friends to meet at a cool belly-dancing lounge, we dressed the part and had an amazing time. This dinner to me was a sort of coming out, it was a pledge in some sense to my new life and my friends were down for it. For those of you out there after experiencing your sadness and when you come up for air, plan a

coming out party either at home or at a

cute lounge or bar and just go with it!

Invite those friends that have

amazing energy, call your Uber and have a

fun and irresponsible night full of tequila

shots and dancing. You may wake up

with a slight hangover but no need to

panic because there is no one at home to

hide from. You can sleep until your

heart's content, wake up, shoot a text to

those that are available to grab brunch

and have an amazing start to your new

life. The next thing I did was really tune

into my emotions when I was doing

things that felt good. For example, I
started getting manicures and pedicures
more often. Instead of going to a
neighborhood spot, I branched out and
found a nicer place that felt like a spa.
Location, location, location.   I was drawn
to pinks, red, blues and yellow polish. I
noticed how the colors on my nails made
me feel enchanted and happier. Like the
color of paint on a wall, I realized pink
and red nails left me beaming and in good
spirits while darker colors made me feel
melancholy. . Finally, I realized how much
I enjoyed eating cake pops and drinking
Chai Lattes while sitting by the window in

my kitchen as the sun set which made me feel very gleeful. I watched people walk past and with each bite or sip I felt warm and fuzzy on the inside, corny I know, but that small gesture changed my mood for the better. I added these moments to my journal and to my gratitude list. I continued to be mindful of my feelings and made an effort to revisit those moments when I felt anxiety and malcontent. Not only did I create new experiences for myself but, I now had a personal toolkit.

So, for those of you out there let's start the process. After the tears have dried out and we are ready for life again, let's start taking inventory of those little affordable things we do daily that bring us joy. Wake up each day and say "Universe or God or *whomever* you acknowledge as your higher power, I'm open and willing to process any old experiences that have gone unnoticed and have any new experiences that can bring me joy today."

Start by being mindful of what you're doing and identifying what the feelings are that are attached to the actions for yourself. Say to yourself "self, today I'm going to treat you to a delicious manicure and pedicure with beautiful pink polish and find the brightest one you can get and build your excitement around it this time.

Or grab yourself an amazing cup of coffee and with every sip acknowledge its deliciousness with the longest "Yummmmmm!" you can have and feel it in your soul while taking a sip. While you are engaged in these activities be intentional in your feelings, feel your moments and when it feels good say...."wow this is delicious, ummmm this feels good to have someone pampering me I deserve this."

Or, "walking around my
neighborhood actually feels amazing."
Just saying "I'm okay" to myself makes me
feel like I am in a good place.   The
takeaway from this is we must identify for
our higher self these feelings that have
been lying dormant within us because
we've not had this opportunity for some
time now so we gotta wake them up. And,
finally jotting them down and how they
make us feel so we can keep a go to list for
the next time because I promise you there
will be a next time you will need to break
out this list. But, now you have a list of
strategies and it'll make transitions

without your child and day to day stress
less dreadful because you know how to
bring some joy back to your life instantly.

Chapter 2

Purge, rid yourself of
unwanted feelings,
typically giving a sense of
cathartic release.

My morning started off like every other morning for the past three weeks. I stayed in bed watching Grey's Anatomy. During this episode, Meredith lost her Mc Dreamy...again. However, this time was different; she was affected so deeply that she couldn't get out of bed. So, in the midst of her depression, as she was lying in bed, in comes her road dog Christina. The monolog starts with a simple but loaded question "Do you have a feeling?" Meredith replies, "I need something to happen. I need a sign that things are gonna change. I need a reason. I need a reason to get up. I need some hope. *But* in the absence of hope, I need to stay in bed and just feel like I'm gonna die today. There was a long seemingly heartfelt pauses and then Christina stops and without a thought pulls the covers off of her and says "Whatever!!!... Get your Ass out of bed and get to work!!!" And like Meredith, I got my ass up and got to work. I realized I had to work and work hard on this new life and journey that's only about me and no one else.

So I started to dig deep within myself and reflected on whether I thought things *could* get better and if they did what would better *look* like. For me, I envisioned better looking like me attending social events, having dinners at my house just because I felt like it with friends old and new and feeling good in the skin that I'm in. What this meant for me was being able to be free to be me in every way I could; clothing, style, going out without a curfew or having to find a babysitter and cooking or *not*. This reflection helped to push me forward.

I thought "*my son was having fun and doing what he should be doing at the age of 18 in the college of his choice.*" I was *a successful, beautiful, fun and sexy single woman so, why not me?*" I'd started to learn what I liked and what felt good to me. I kept this in my list of *"things about me"* within my phone and in my journal. I got out of the bed and just started to purge. To purge yourself means to rid yourself of unwanted or negative feelings, conditions or memories that you are attached to. A purge is a cutting off, clearing out of all the things that are uncertain within your life. Get rid of things that exacerbate your bad feelings. Those pants that make you feel and look like you still have your baby weight, that sweater that's ugly as hell but it's comfortable, those shoes that has a heal that resembles a sneaker that married a boot....throw it all in the bag and head over to Goodwill immediately. Take the unsexy underwear that fit like old granny's panties...and you feel so unsexy when you take them out to wear but without thought you put them on...toss then in the garbage. Burn them, do what you need to do to get rid of them, because news flash, they make underwear that are sexy, pretty and comfortable and also affordable.

I started my purge with the junk food in my in my kitchen. I knew this was the easiest place to start. I started with all the junk food I accumulated over the years that kept my son happy but made me gain a few extra pounds. I then purged my bathroom and linen closets of all the Superman, Batman and He-Man bandages that were lost in the crevices. I cleaned out the tooth brushes, lotions and men's sprays that he had left behind which only had an ounce left in the bottle. I also noticed that there were items deep inside that my ex left when we separated such as colognes, toothbrushes etc. so I tossed those as well; which felt really good.

After I completed walking through the kitchen and bathroom throwing things away, I moved on to my bedroom closet. The closet was a jungle, *literally* a jungle...every pattern existed in there from every era I had lived through. I had cheetah print, leopard print and a mix of both...why Lord why? I had clothes from previous years that were too big from losing weight, too dumpy, too small from gaining weight and too old and not my style at this age. When I tell you I had items in my closet that should've been left on Walmart's sale rack but I bought it because it was shirt for $2 and who could pass that up. Not I apparently!

I took everything out and laid it on the bed. I then tried on every item whether it was clothing, shoes or accessories I'd ever owned and made three piles. So, I know you're thinking this sounds like a lot, and it is, but it's what hope looks like. It's what brings that feeling of possibility back into your life, it's ultimately what getting your ASS up and getting to work look and feels like. In essence doing these small acts of kindness for yourself will bring the feeling of possibility back into your life.

The closet is the resting place for the past, present and future *you*.

Everything you have ever experienced lives within your clothing. Your clothing holds on to more memories than you can imagine. You can quickly turn a bad mood around with every garment you put on, every color you put on and every shoe that fits perfectly with an outfit.

My three piles were labeled a *(1) maybe I like, (2) what the hell was I thinking when I brought this pile and (3) yessss girl this is where this was hiding.* After I created these piles I bagged up donations for the Salvation Army because one *recreated woman's* junk is another *recreated woman's* treasure. So I blessed my bag of donated clothes with hopes

that these clothes will bring joy to

someone's life and dropped it off at my

local donation center. I got a bottle of

wine, came back home to now try on all

the new found treasures I came across

with different pieces to see what new

sexy fun outfits I could create. I pulled

out necklaces, earrings and bracelets that

became my staple pieces. I listed a few

pieces I could add that would just bring it

all together such as a long flowing

sweater, a few silk button down shirts in

a beautiful shade of coral and of course a

cute pair of skinny jeans because why

not…who can't use a cute pair of skinny jeans? A quick makeover can take any work outfit from day to night instantly for those nights when you know you'll meet friends for a drink after work.

I then sorted items in my closet by camisoles and sleeveless shirts, skirts, dresses and pants. If you want to get really fancy sort your clothes by colors and seasons. A small adjustment will give your closet life, but for me, I just took it by categories because by this time I was exhausted and all of my wine was gone. I was also a little drunk by this time but either way I was running on fumes. I added one more step to my organization routine, because I have an eighteen year old and my memory is shot. I took pictures to be printed the next day of outfits and tapped them inside my closet door so when I got ready for work or a night out with the ladies it would make it easy to just grab items and go.

The next day when I woke up I sat and reflected on the entire purging process. I felt like I was starting to grow wings. This new found energy made me feel like a butterfly that had just come out of cocoon. I thought about the process of metamorphosis and how the caterpillar's body dies and a new body forms inside a protective shell known as a chrysalis. The Chrysalis is the transformation stage between the larva also known as the juvenile stage and the adult stage. The cocoon stage is equivalent to our grieving stage; it is a major life transition and everyone goes through it.

This stage happens after our children have gone off to college or our relationship with someone has ended; it happens in any transition that's serious enough to alter our definition of self. We get into a stage where our body just wants to comfort itself; shed its old layers of hurtful memories and circumstances and become a new creature. This cycle for most can be hard and it requires that you have hope that life can get better, it requires a desire to be in that better space and the openness to try new things. It requires us to get our "Ass" up and get to work on helping our bodies to shed itself of the old mommy layers of clothing and sad feelings. Let's get up!!!

Chapter 3

A creation of new
routines; to produce or
bring about by a course of
action or behavior.

In the episode of the season I was watching of Grey's Anatomy, Meredith said it best, "And sometimes what we want is exactly what we need...but sometimes what we need is a new plan." I thought I've cried a river and was well on my way but realized I hit a bump. In the past I've looked to friends and family for support and turned up with a few unwanted gifts such as pottery classes but I still felt empty and was trying to fill a void and take ownership over my life. I finished purging my closet of all unflattering, old unwanted items and now

I needed to take more matters into my own hands and create a new plan.

I jotted down my daily routines from the time I woke up until I went back to sleep and breathed in a sigh of despair because my life still felt boring as hell. *Even though* I was now cute as hell with my new outfits I've been creating...I was in the laundromat on a Friday night and I was turning down invites to happy hour. I looked in the mirror and saw a young woman who felt vibrant, fun and sexy but I constantly got home by 6pm and got under the covers by 7:30pm. Now I'm not saying that these things aren't ok but your life should not be one that's filled with chores and no real joyous interest insight. I decided to change up the routine. I moved a few pieces of furniture around in my bedroom and living room to signify "Change Is Here!" Sidebar this can help at any time you're feeling like things are too much of the same or mundane.)... Move around a few pieces in the room, change your sheets and put a new duvet cover on the bed maybe add fresh flowers. Your living space starts to feel refreshed and new again. I then re-acquainted myself with my neighborhood bars and restaurants.

I knew bars and cafes were popping up all over Brooklyn and now I had a reason to bring friends to patronize the local hot spots. I decided to start by putting together a happy hour of my own with my friends for one midweek event...and followed that up with a Saturday bar experience in Brooklyn at a cool whiskey place that had games and good music for some dancing. I was so proud of myself for not falling asleep on my co-workers but also for stepping outside the box and going out with friends on a Saturday evening instead of folding laundry or meal prepping. I actually left my meal prep for Mondays and this became my sure fire routine day.

Prepping meals for one person became easier with time, however, one night a week I treated myself to a fancy meal at a restaurant that caught my attention as I traveled to and from work. I took a book just in case I felt weird and needed to bury my head and not make eye contact with the couples on dates. But as I got more comfortable eating out alone I realized I didn't need a book. I noticed there were at least four other single people having dinner alone so I held my head high and ordered my second glass of wine a raised my glass to the sky with pride and cheers to gratefulness. After dinner, I actually walked home and reflected on the experience. Choosing to dine alone was Empowering and apparently a very common occurrence in my neighborhood.

The next week I walked into a new bar that'd opened by my house and sat at the bar terrified. I felt that I would be looked at as a poor sap but I ordered a glass of wine anyways. As I sat and sipped from my glass the bar started to fill up with people. They sat next to me and started to talk about their day; work traumas and what life looked like for them and I engaged. It was such a nice experience...it helped me to understand that people just really want companionship and authentic relationships no matter how long or short of a time we listen and share. I asked the bartender if this was a norm and he said yes! He explained that on an average weekday many people come in just to talk and not to be home alone. This became my new favorite place...they held game nights and I was able to meet my neighbors, even at the most depressing times like the holidays I could find friendship here.

I finally accepted the invitations from my co-workers which opened so many new experiences for me. My coworkers were connected to various "meet-up" groups around New York City and invited me to tag along. I became a new social butterfly and everyday was different. So my advice to you, after you've cried, grieved and purged let's reimagine a new life.

Start by writing down what you could possibly enjoy if given the opportunity and unlimited finances. Then create a calendar and make these events a priority. Let's start doing some of these things after work not only on Saturdays and Sundays but during the week. Start by doing 1-2 new things while also including coworkers or neighbors so you can start to build a support system that's in close proximity to you. Create a new circle of friends with other single women and men that can make you smile and feel re-energized about life. By becoming a part of a meet-up group such as those found on Meetup.com. This is a social site that contains all types of fun meetup groups from brunch and movies at the Angelika Theatre or Salsa lessons at a local Latin

Club. These meet ups happen daily and weekly and many contain the same group of people at each meet up so you get use to the faces you see and can create authentic relationships.

This stage is all about creation and new experiences and more importantly doing things that are fun for you!

Chapter 4

Holiday hearts...not so
cheery.

It's the holidays and I'm scared as hell of what my home will look like as a single woman with no one to come home to because of how my life has gone over this last year. I am still single and my son will be coming home for the holidays but the preparation is all on me. My sadness came when I started to reminisce about my son when he was younger and we shared in the excitement of buying a Christmas tree with decorations to match. We talked about what we did to prepare for the holidays. We planned the menu and cooked the most delicious Latin dishes and desserts from recipes my aunt sent me throughout the years. We had family and friends over some evenings and made Coquito which is a Latin drink that has lots of rum, sweet milk and spices. Coquito is similar to a spiked eggnog drink. We put the drink in nice bottles to give to family and friends as a gift along with cookies. I loved to bake cookies for the kids on holidays. We made stockings and hung them by the tree and hid our gifts until it was 12am and both my son and I would sneak in to put our gifts inside so we could find them in the morning when we woke up. On Christmas Day we would go to my family's house after we shared in our own festivities at our home so we could exchange gifts and have dinner with the family.

Now holidays aren't the same with him away. Buying and decorating the tree seemed so sad to do alone and the anticipation of it made me feel like such a loser. It actually made me realize more than anything that I was still single and that the house was truly empty. For the first year he was away I just reverted back to my Netflix shell. My Netflix shell aka Grey's Anatomy is always the evidence that I am depressed and feeling like everything sucks in life. I watch Grey's Anatomy so I don't have to face the reality that is happening outside of my doors. I watch it so I can escape the shit storm of sadness that is happening in my life and this was where I was at once again in my life. I watched this until Christmas Day came and as soon as I woke up I couldn't bare being alone so I got dressed and went to my family's house. Don't get me wrong he was of course home for the holidays during breaks from school but for the little time he was home we exchanged gifts then he was off to visit his father, grandparents and friends he hadn't seen since going away. When the holidays was over I was so relieved but still not the happiest.

The next year I decided that I couldn't just wait around for the New Year to roll in and more than that I couldn't let another year catch me in a sad space wishing for something to happen and making Meredith and Christina my best friends. Meredith said at the end of an episode "life is the most fragile unstable unpredictable thing there is...in fact there's only one thing about life we can be sure of...it ain't over til it's over" and with this I thought to myself that I had done so much work to get out of my funk and I couldn't stop now. I couldn't let this feeling of unpredictability keep me down. I had to once again start creating the life that I wanted even through the holidays and I had to do it with some excitement in my heart even if I didn't know what the hell was coming. I was going to go with it. I started with the thought that I was going to go back to having holiday celebrations but for the adults that have no small kids and are living in this same funk. I thought to myself this could be the start of my own sort of holiday traditions because guess what once college is over for him life will begin and things are not going to go back to the way they were before he left so it's time to think about what my future would look like without anyone in my home with me. What would I want the holidays to feel like when he's off with his own family and friends creating his holiday traditions?

I started with buying me the most unique tree I could find. It was fun and glamorous. I was made without actual tree leaves. It was silver and made from garland; think of a magical sparkly silver tree that shined without any added ornaments. The best part about it is that it was $5 at the Dollar Tree. It sparkled so much it didn't even need lights which was great for me because I wanted an easy clean up and not to spend an hour decorating a tree and unraveling Christmas lights. You'll notice that when your kids go off to college you actually become the person that wants no fuss in things and are often the person who doesn't give a shit if things are less perfect....these things matter less. I found a beautiful Christmas tree skirt and created stockings to match for he and I. I then planned a Christmas Eve game night for friends and family members who could make it. We played games like gestures and charades to add everyone in. I completed the evening with all the Latin dishes I use to create and Coquito was the star along with wines brought by those that came and instead of us buying each person a gift we played "dirty Santa" which is a fun game that get adults back into the selfish child like Christmas spirit we knew as kids.

For those of you who don't know what dirty Santa is; it's a game where each person brings a gender neutral gift. Each person gets the opportunity to choose a number from a hat and the

person with the highest number let's say

10 is the highest number they get to

choose their gift first without opening it.

The next person with the number right

below which is the number 9 gets to

choose either from the pile of gifts or they

can choose, snatch or rip the gift from the

person who went before in fun of course

and without any bloodshed. This happens

all the way down to the person who has

the number one. The number one gets to

take their pick from everyone before

them or take the last gift on the table. In

the end we each open the gifts together to

see what they either gave up or got stolen from them during the game. This brings on so much laughter and the gifts are extremely funny as well because when you say gender neutral you get 15 lotto tickets or an "I love farting" mug. This new Christmas tradition became one of my new favorites I still do now.

Since I worked in a school I was off for some time so to keep me out of the funk I planned to meet up with friends during the days for lunch of course but I added some other new adventures to continue to create new traditions. Ice skating was on the list at our neighborhood ice skating rink and that was followed with Hot Toddies to warm us up at a local bar. A potluck at one of friend's house was another event along with a visit to the Christmas tree in Rockefeller center at night with a group of friends who were able to meet us there with a nice dinner to follow. Before you knew it my week had gone by, I hadn't reverted back to my Grey's Anatomy shell and New Year Eve was here and that was spent with my neighbors and a few bottles of Prosecco as we watched the ball drop. I realized that prior to this I had put so much pressure on how I was going to spend my holidays as opposed to what I would like to feel like during the holiday season. I wanted to feel comforted by good friends and family it didn't matter the amount of people but the energy of those who were around me at this moment mattered most. I wanted to feel joy and visiting all the places that I had during this time brought joy and laughter. I removed the fear of me being alone and opened up my heart to share these feelings with others and understood that around the holidays many people are trying to create a sense of comfort and joy

and they welcome outings and potluck
dinners to equally help them get through.

These traditions became my
traditions and I no longer felt fear as the
next three years of my son's college
career went by. I felt excitement for the
holidays and knew that ice-skating would
be on my menu along with dates with
friends, New York City lights at night and
shiny Christmas trees that would
complete my holiday festivities. So I
charge you to create a new holiday
tradition for yourself. If you're anything
like me you're probably dreading this and
have reverted back to your favorite show

or movie so shut that off and grab a pen and paper. Sit down and write the feelings that you want to have during this holiday season. Create a list of things you would want to do either alone or with friends just because you can such as my list; ice skating and hot toddies. Or in the summer wine and a nice beach day. Then find a friend or two that can do some of these with you. It doesn't need to be the same friend *all the time* and you don't need to be best buds they just have to be willing to go with the flow and have a good day without any negative talk. If this fails check out NYC Meetup groups or post on your Facebook page where you want to go and find new groups of people that are already doing this activity or want to attend and let them join in.

The point of the matter is that there are no real rules on how to get these activities done just get them done because this is about creating new traditions.

Let's create a Holiday heart filled with joy!

Chapter 5

A good time to start
something new...

When my son was an adolescent, I enrolled in school and worked on my bachelors and master's degree. I remember the hustle of taking him to school each day, having a sitter pick him up after school, then dropping him to his father's house. Finally, at the end of the evening I'd picked him up from his father's house and travel home. We did this all over again each day; the drop off and pick up regimen until the summer. I was exhausted many days. Other days when I sat in class I felt as though I wasn't retaining as much information as I should be. I also felt as though I didn't get the best possible education which was not because of my professor or my schools negligence but because I was always multitasking. My list of desires never stopped growing but somethings were outweighed and became less of a priority. Some desires or even curious possible endeavors such as my desire to become a floral designer was of course not a high priority with the price tag on classes and the lack of time I had to take *the* classes...it just didn't pan out.

When I first gave birth to my son, I immediately knew that I was a creative person. I wanted to become a chef. I wanted to design and create meals that looked as though they were from the most exquisite restaurants. One morning I woke up and I decided that I was tired of my regular desk job and I took the train into Manhattan, took a tour of a culinary school and decided this was for me. I was so excited. I took a step in the direction that would empower me and help me to fulfill my dreams; I was excited about my decision. I couldn't wait to talk about this with my family. When I got back on the train I was still on a high from the tour of the school. I sat down and decided to think about how I was going to pay for this new experience. I then looked at the new class schedule and my heart dropped. Class ended at ten o'clock each night four days a week. I had to complete a semester long internship in a restaurant.

It sounded great but this schedule threw a monkey wrench in my plan. The thing about restaurants is they close at the wee hours of the night. As a dedicated mother, I was not willing to sacrifice the little time I had with my son each evening to follow a desire that will always put me in a situation where I would need to choose motherhood over a fun career. So

I had to once again put that on the back burner and turned to a career that gave me the freedom to get home at a reasonable hour. This happened to me a few times as he grew and matured in his own endeavors. My desires got pushed back so far in my head that I didn't think of them anymore. I thought about my career in the same way I took on motherhood; stable and predictable. I wasn't satisfied in my career. I had this urge to explore and experience the things I once couldn't because I wanted to create a stable life for my son.

I remembered a quote that I once had on my mirror and it said "and suddenly you know...it's time to start something new and trust the magic of beginnings." With this inspiration, I once again went back to my journal and created a list of career ventures that I once found to be fulfilling and fun. I also listed career choices or endeavors that I have always been curious about but either couldn't afford to attend or didn't have time to do. I found that I liked interior designing. I loved learning how to encourage healing through spiritual, emotional and physical wellness. I learned to teach clients nutrition, exercise and learning how to tap into one's higher self through meditation. I decided since I now have the time I can take classes within each one of these areas to get a better understanding of how they can be incorporated into a career. I found a few donation based classes at my local yoga studio such as Yoga for the People that allows the community to experience yoga on a love offering. I researched nutritional benefits when I had down time at work and visited a few community based wellness meetups from Meetups.com. These meetings helped me to start to understand how to incorporate more nutritional elements into my diet. I reached out to a few friends that hosted or visited a free new moon meditation workshop and I started to make this a priority so I could learn to mediate and experience the benefits of it. I was careful to stay on a budget and didn't want a membership of any kind because I was still in the exploration phase. But, I also changed the way I looked at these new experiences. I was conscious to see them not only as a possible career shift but a way to build community and create a project that gave me something to do when I didn't want to go to the bar or out to dinner with friends.

These community experiences gave me a space to unwind and quiet my mind and create an energy of excitement when those little spurts of sadness and unpredictability in what my future would look like came on. All of these new experiences allowed me to branch off into a new business venture which was opening my private Psychotherapy practice. Within my practice I was able to use all of what I had now learned over the last 3 to 6 months. I teach and train clients to heal past trauma through mindfulness practices, breath-work and oil healing.

My son leaving for college allowed me the time to explore new opportunities but my willingness to start something new and trust the magic of new beginnings gave me the courage to get out of my own way. I stopped thinking "I'm too old to start something new, I don't have the money or I don't know where to find these community programs." I used the support of those around me to find these places and I asked friends for resources. The most important thing is that I changed my perspective. I changed my mindset from "let's just have fun" to "let's experience some of things that we always wanted to do but couldn't afford because of time or other circumstances."

So my friends, this is the time for you to start to brainstorm in your journal. Write down all of your dreams, wishes, wants and desires. List the ventures, activities and desires you had when your children were at home and you had to put them on the back burner. In your journal draw a heart on a page and fill it with ten things you'd imagine doing if money or time was not an obstacle. It's the time to think outside the box and explore activities. Here is a list that you can consider:

1. If you wanted to be a chef take a trip to the culinary school. Take a tour and see if this feels fun and like something you may want to do. Find out if you can visit on a day when class is in session. Look into meet-up groups that cook together and attend a group.

2. If you want to become a Floral Designer contact your local Botanical Garden

and take a free or low cost class to get a better understanding of what this will feel like. Ask your local florist can you volunteer sometime in the evenings to gage whether this could be a good fit for you.

3. If your desire is to go back to school to further your education or gain your first degree, then start this process by searching what major you would want to explore. Find the school

online or take a tour and

create a calendar of

deadlines and

requirements. Look into a

community college or even

dream bigger and get into a

four year college you may

have been dreaming of

before motherhood. Look

into the application process

and apply.

The time is now! It's time to start

something new and trust the magic of this

new beginning. You deserve it and you

earned it!!!!!

Chapter 6

For once in my life...for once...I am doing something in my life that is only for me...

As I started to get comfortable with living a life that put my needs at the forefront I realized that this could actually be the start of something new. Of course I thought of an episode where Lexi Grey, Meredith's little sister was having sex with Alex Karev after her break up from Mc Steamy and Meredith of course thought this was trashy and approached Lexi about it. Lexi said to Meredith after being asked why was she having sex with Karev "for once in my life...for once...I am doing something that is only for me..." This was the way I felt about my transition to an empty nest. I was having fun and learning how to be my best self.

I discovered my likes and dislikes. Most importantly, I realized I was learning that if I wasn't my best self than I couldn't be the best for anyone else. I fell in love with the new me. This feeling of euphoria was too infectious not to share with a companion at some point. I started to feel like I loved this new person and wanted to spend more time with me and a companion at some point.

I realized I been through so much over this last year with exploring and discovering that I discovered who I was at the core. When I stripped myself of being just a mom, I noticed that I had been through so much over the last year. I decided to date myself and create a list of non-negotiables for my soon to be mate. I know it sounds weird but *hey* I went with it because if you would have asked me earlier this year what I would be doing when my son went to college it would not have been all of these amazing things I have done.

This year I cried, cried and cried some more. I allowed myself to feel my emotions and grieved the loneliness I felt. I created new regimens that brought love, joy and excitement into my life. I discovered self-care tools that took my emotional, physical and spiritual wellness to a new level. I created new friendships and no longer was the woman who ran straight home after work I now had a supportive group of friends that met for game nights at my local pub. Things were going so well for me and it was time to date so I started with dating myself.

Yes people... I started to date myself. I was a gorgeous woman who wanted to learn to be madly in love with myself before adding someone to this equation. When I thought about it I was no longer the person I was before this journey started. I was now a beautiful, successful woman *and* mother. I was no longer just noticing myself as a mom. I was standing on my own. I wasn't sad or depressed and I was living my best life. This was only the beginning. More Most importantly, I didn't want to ever go back to that lowly place I was in after my son had gone off to college, my relationship ended and my dog died; basically when life seemed to be over.

I felt like I mattered more than anything in this world. I knew my worth. I was ready to fall in love with myself so, I could attract a like-minded person to fall in love with me. I started with thinking about how I would treat someone that I was in love with. ? I thought about what would be some of the things I would want to do for them. I wondered what would quality time looked like with spent with someone I loved looked like. I came up with a few activities but felt a little weird when I realized this task was all about me.

I wasn't comfortable with so much attention which is why this was a perfect activity. This was about me giving myself more love than I've ever experienced at one time. I thought about all the progress

I made throughout the year and decided to go with it. I mean what's the worst that could happen? I wouldn't treat myself to dinner again. That was impossible as much as I loved to eat. I started my *"date myself"* journey with finding an amazing lobster dinner recipe for 2. I was eating alone but who turns down lobster leftovers? I sent the most beautiful flowers to my office and signed the card "you are truly loved by me!" I then purchased a delicious bottle of wine and put on a nice dress when I got home. I did it up because I wanted to actually feel like I was on a date. I lit a candle played a nice music toon and sat alone with myself and enjoyed this amazing evening.

The following week, I decided that next week I was going to I treated myself to a movie. This was date number two. 2. I picked out a movie, and yes sent myself flowers again and so that I could carry my flowers as I walked to my movie. I treated myself to all of the popcorn and candy I could eat. I enjoyed the movie, especially walking in with the flowers that I sent myself. I turned heads and heard whispers as I strolled in with the biggest grin on my face. Could they tell I was happy? Did other women aspire to be happy like me? The most fattening movie foods and sat and enjoyed my movie. After a few of these single dates I began to notice what made me feel happy and feel loved. Started to feel like I knew how it would feel to be treated with such love and desire. I turned everyday activities y into a solo date. I would do alone into a date with myself. From shopping for groceries, getting a manicure to walking around in my neighborhood; everything was done with flare and pizzazz and ended with a glass of wine.

I went shopping and stopped off and purchased myself a glass of wine and tapas. If I went to the nail salon I stopped at a beautiful restaurant and added a meal to this. Some days I woke up and planned a day of just me time which consisted of a walk on the Brooklyn Promenade, a stop at a flea market and a glass of Chardonnay. Doing this for myself now taught me what to expect from others when I started to date. I learned that I had to put limits on the things that didn't bring me joy. I also learned that being alone doesn't mean I have to be lonely. This also taught me that *just because you are by yourself doesn't mean you are alone or lonely.* I was close to the finish line of this journey. I knew that this was one of my final steps in my journey. I learned to come home at night and sit in my own thoughts without fear. This helped me I began to incorporate meditation into my self-care tool kit. I no longer looked at others as they walked past me in the streets with envy or sadness. I embraced my thoughts without fear. I could now smile with them because I smiled because I knew what how they felt in their joy. Here are a few gems that stuck with me throughout this process:

1. Celebrate yourself

2. Love yourself

3. Take care of yourself

   mentally and emotionally

I learned what true love of self was

which was giving yourself the best you

had to offer. I begin to celebrate myself

within this for being a great mother who

sacrificed her life so that my son could be

his best self. I praised myself instead of

feeling sorry for myself. I knew that for

once in my life...for once...I was doing

something in my life that is only for me

and it felt so darn good...and this was only

the beginning!

I challenge you to begin to celebrate yourself. Start by dating yourself. Take yourself to dinner with a gorgeous dress on or create the most amazing meal at home and go the extra mile with desert, music and a candle. Send flowers to yourself with a beautiful note attached. Incorporate dates into your week so you too can for once...do something in your life that is only for you!

Chapter 7

Change is the only
constant...

Change is the only constant in all of science... energy...matter...it's always changing morphing, merging, growing and dying. It's the way people try not to change that's unnatural... the way we cling to what things were not to what they are now... the way we cling to old memories instead of forming new ones... the way we insist on believing despite every scientific indication that anything in this lifetime is permanent. Change is constant...how we experience change that's up to us. It can feel like death or it can feel like a second chance at life if we open our fingers loosen our grips, go with it. Change can be a shot of pure adrenalin that propels us into feeling invincible.

I remember the moment that my son got the acceptance letter and moved upstate to attend school. I am so proud that he accomplished one of the greatest things that we hoped and dreamed for our kids. Even though he cleared this major milestone in his life, I fell apart and felt lost. I literally crawled into a fetal position and cried for months. I spent eighteen years living my life for him. I made every decision based on what was best for him. I forgot about my hopes and dreams and lived a life that no longer included me. I was Mark's mother and my identity was him. Don't get me wrong I'm so grateful that I had the opportunity to be his mom. I'm grateful that I was in a space to nurture a young man that is caring, compassionate and full of life. But when I dropped him off at his dream school, I had no idea who I was. I didn't know what was in store for me. I was lost and *I knew it* and these feelings are so normal to have. We don't realize that they are and many of us have been in this same space or will be at some point. . We hide and hold on to these feelings of sadness and a since of abandonment instead of allowing the grieving process to start. We move into a depression which hinders our progress and many times we give up and allow life to pass us by.

I couldn't let this happen. I didn't want my son to look at the woman he admires and say "what happened to you?" I had to get up one day and *"get my life"* as they say. I had to discover my new self and let go of my old self because that person didn't serve me anymore. That person was afraid of new experiences and had given up on her desires. Through this journey I have learned that I don't have to make all of my decisions *final* decisions. I can make a decision for today and tomorrow another if I choose to do so. I realize that I get to choose what I want every time all the time. I don't have to live the way society has deemed fit.

I sent my son off to college and began a new life. I created new possibilities where there seemed to be no possibilities in site. I tried everything once and if I enjoyed it and it brought me good emotions I put it on my list for future endeavors. I relied on my journal because after all was said and done I needed a place to reflect and share my praises. I got outside my comfort zone and allowed myself to be in the moment each time I attempted something new and allowed it to turn out to be just that...an experience. I loved on myself through this journey. I was kind to myself and allowed myself to just be in the moment each time I had moments.

This chapter started like all the others in this book with a quote from the show that kept me company in one of my toughest times. The quote came about when Christina got married and Meredith was trying to have a baby. All of this happened after the hospital had a huge shooting and everyone's lives were different. She talks about change being the most natural thing in life. She states "It's the way people try not to change that's unnatural... the way we cling to what things were *not* to what they are now... the way we cling to old memories instead of forming new ones.

We can't fight change, it's unnatural and unhealthy and literally hurts us more than any break up or loss in our lives. If we don't allow change we die inside slowly. My favorite part of this quote is when she states that "Change is constant how we experience change that's up to us!" It's totally up to us in how we want to go through this process. If we want to get to the other side which for some may mean a life full of community, laughter and joy than we have to choose to form new memories, experience new things and not cling to what we thought our lives were supposed to look like.

Finally she says change can feel like death or it can feel like a second chance at life if we open our fingers loosen our grips, go with it... it can feel like pure adrenalin...like at any moment we can have another chance at life...like at any moment we can be born all over again!!! Sending our children off to college and coming home to an *Empty Nest* can feel like death. Our hearts are lonely and we are lost. But the moment we reach out to friends and create new regimens, rituals and experiences it can feel like a second chance at life!

Change is the *only* constant and how *WE* experience change that's all up to us!!!

Thank you for experiencing this journey with me...may your Empty Nest be as sexy as my house became when I opened my fingers loosened my grip and went with it... it feels like pure adrenalin...and at every moment I get to have another chance at life!!!

Printed in Great Britain
by Amazon